Level B Boo__ _

Dr. Funster's
THINK-A-MINUTES

Fast, Fun Brainwork
for Higher Grades
and Top Test Scores

Titles in the series:
Dr. Funster's Think-A-Minutes

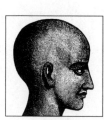

© 2002
CRITICAL THINKING BOOKS & SOFTWARE
www.CriticalThinking.com
P.O. Box 448 • Pacific Grove • CA 93950-0448
Phone 800-458-4849
ISBN 0-89455-809-9
Printed in the United States of America

About Dr. Funster's Think-A-Minutes

This collection of fast, fun riddles, puzzles, and teasers develops thinking skills for higher grades and top test scores. The activities are perfect for school, home, and travel. They are very popular as brain-start, extra credit, sponge, or reward activities.

This collection is taken from a variety of past and current books published by Critical Thinking Books & Software. If you would like to see more of a particular type of activity, refer to page 46 for other pages with similar activities in this book or for the names of the series from which the activities were taken.

For other books with similar activities, call 800-458-4849 for the store nearest you or to order directly.

Mystery Shape

1. Inside the largest circle, write the numeral for the total number of shapes.

2. If your first answer is spelled with four letters, shade in the small triangle. If it's not, cross out the last two shapes.

3. The shape you are looking for has only straight lines.

4. Cross out the largest of each shape.

5. Cross out the shape that has fewer than four sides.

6. Cross out the shape that does not have equal sides.

7. Put the number 1 above the mystery shape.

It's a Date!

November	S	M	T	W	T	F	S
	1	2	3	4	5	6	7
	8	9	10	11	12	13	14
	15	16	17	18	19	20	21
	22	23	24	25	26	27	28
	29	30					

1. What is the date of the third Wednesday of the month? _____

2. Name the two days that occur five times this month.

   _____ _____

3. What is the date of the second Monday after the second Tuesday?

   _____

4. What is the date two days after the fourth Friday? _____

5. What day of the week will it be on December 1? _____

6. What day of the week was October 31? _____

The Color of Fun

DIRECTIONS: Color this map with the least number of colors possible. No areas side by side may have the same color.

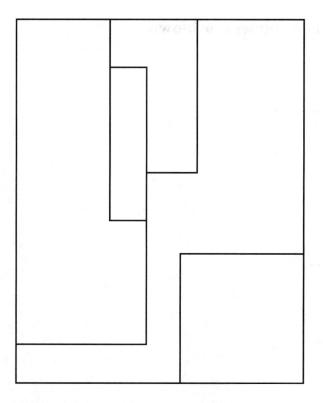

1. What is the least number of colors you can use? _____

2. Create another map for which you need more colors.

Word Maker

DIRECTIONS: Add a letter or letters to either end of the **last** word in the word sequence to form a new word.

Example: low, blow, **blower or blown**

1. in, pain, _____

2. or, ore, _____

3. ad, mad, _____

4. on, one, _____

5. at, ate, _____

6. it, fit, _____

From *Verbal Sequences. A1.* For more activities like the one above, call 800-458-4849 for the store nearest you or to order directly. © 2002 Critical Thinking Books & Software • www.criticalthinking.com

Think Literally!

DIRECTIONS: This verbal puzzle is really a common phrase. Write the phrase in the blanks below.

EXAMPLE: | STAND ME | means **Stand By Me** since **Stand** is next to (by) **Me**.

_____   _____

_____   _____

Squares and More Squares

How many squares can you find below?

From *Classroom Quickies Book 3*. For more activities like the one above, call 800-458-4849 for the store nearest you or to order directly. © 2002 Critical Thinking Books & Software · www.criticalthinking.com

Turn the Triangles

1.

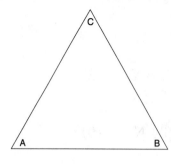

Turn the triangle clockwise one time in your head. Write the new positions of the letters in the triangle at the right.

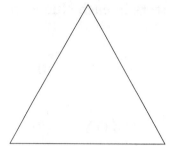

2.

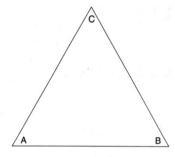

Turn the triangle counterclockwise twice in your head. Write the new positions of the letters in the triangle at the right.

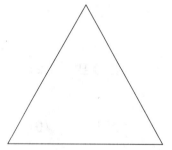

3.

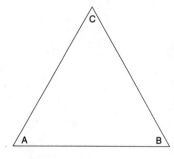

Turn the triangle clockwise three times in your head. Write the new positions of the letters in the triangle at the right.

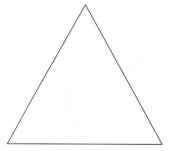

Word Puzzlers

DIRECTIONS: For each of the three puzzles below, find a three-letter word that fits with the clue words. The answer must be a real word. Avoid names (such as AMY) and words with repeating letters (such as EGG). The letters in parentheses show how many letters in each clue word are in the final answer.

1. PIG	(0)	2. PIE	(0)	3. DAY	(2)
JOY	(2)	MEN	(2)	TIN	(0)
BAR	(1)	NOT	(1)	ANT	(1)
KEY	(1)	MOP	(1)	LID	(2)
SOB	(2)	JAM	(2)	OIL	(1)
NUT	(0)	FLY	(0)	DIP	(1)

_____   _____   _____

From *Creative Problem Solving Activities Book A1.* For more activities like the one above, call 800-458-4849 for the store nearest you or to order directly. © 2002 Critical Thinking Books & Software • www.criticalthinking.com

All Aboard!

DIRECTIONS: Look at the graphic below. You're looking to find out when the train is able to reach Dallas. Then, based on the light patterns shown for each route, write YES if the train can pass or NO if it cannot pass. The first one has been done for you.

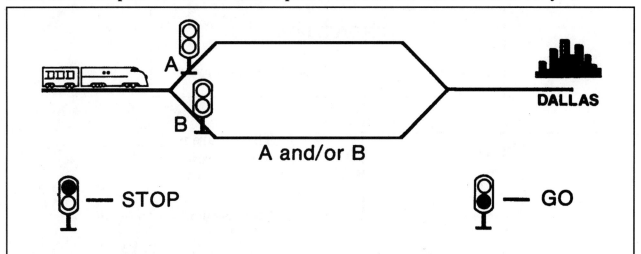

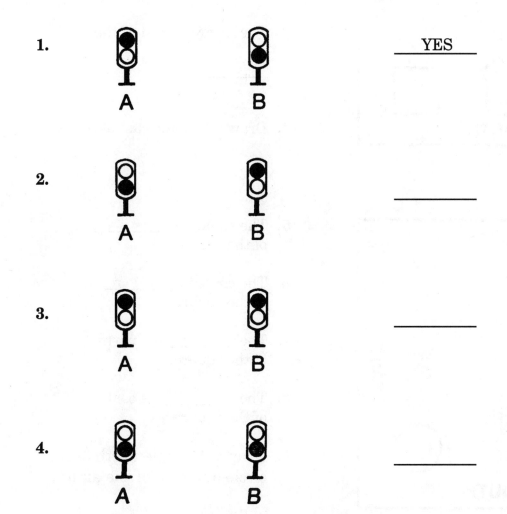

1. _____ YES _____

2. _____

3. _____

4. _____

From *Visual Logic: Disjunction* For more activities like the one above, call 800-458-4849
for the store nearest you or to order directly. © 2002 Critical Thinking Books & Software • www.criticalthinking.com   9

North, South, East, and West

DIRECTIONS: Select the word from the Choice Box that correctly completes the sentences below. Draw the figures as instructed.

CHOICE BOX

arrow, circle, east, north, south, square, west

---

1. The square is _____ of the arrow.

2. The arrow is south of the _____ .

3. The arrow is west of the _____ .

4. Draw a triangle east of the circle.

5. The square is _____ of the arrow.

6. The circle is _____ of the square.

7. The _____ is north of the square.

8. The _____ is east of the square.

9. Draw a triangle north of the circle and east of the arrow.

From *Thinking Directionally Book B1.* For more activities like the one above, call 800-458-4849 for the store nearest you or to order directly. © 2002 Critical Thinking Books & Software • www.criticalthinking.com

What's Really Important

DIRECTIONS: Royce wanted a pet dog. His parents said no. He asked again later. They said he'd have to give them some good reasons to have a dog before they'd let him have one. Circle all of Royce's statements that are relevant to what his parents said.

a. All of my friends have dogs.

b. A lot of U.S. Presidents have had dogs.

c. I want a dog.

d. It will teach me responsibility.

e. It will keep me company.

f. It will protect me in case strangers come around.

g. It will give me something to show off to the other kids.

h. If I can't have a dog, then I'd like to have a cat.

i. Someone famous once said, "Every boy should have a dog."

Words That Match

DIRECTIONS: Draw a line from the phrase in the left column to a related rhyming word pair in the right column.

Phrase	**Think link**
1. a stone watch	blue flu
2. a large hog	toad road
3. a trout plate	rock clock
4. a soggy airplane	star jar
5. a rodent's home	fire tire
6. a color disease	big pig
7. frog street	wet jet
8. a sun container	mouse house
9. a burning wheel	neat street
10. a tidy road	fish dish

From *Language Smarts Book A1*. For more activities like the one above, call 800-458-4849 for the store nearest you or to order directly. © 2002 Critical Thinking Books & Software • www.criticalthinking.com

Get Your Brain in Gear

DIRECTIONS: The sheets of paper drawn below are to be folded along the dotted lines. In the space to the right of each sheet, describe or draw a picture of how that sheet will look after it has been folded.

1.

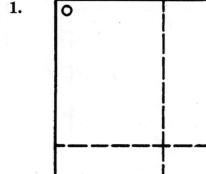

2.

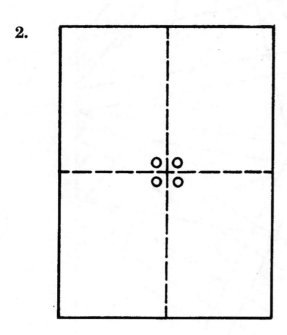

Toothbrush Detective

DIRECTIONS: Somewhere in the picture below is a toothbrush just like the one at right. (The one below is bigger!) Find the larger toothbrush and trace it.

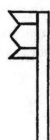

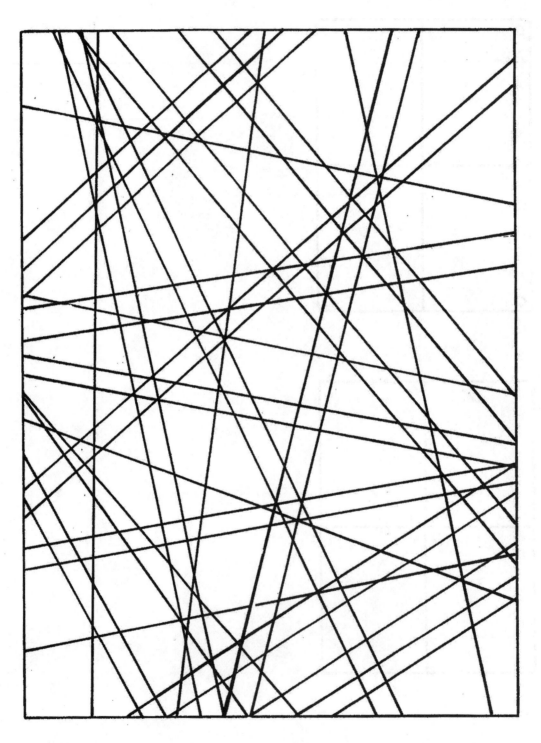

From *Brain Stretchers Book 1.* For more activities like the one above, call 800-458-4849 for the store nearest you or to order directly. © 2002 Critical Thinking Books & Software • www.criticalthinking.com

What Comes Next?

DIRECTIONS: Draw the figure that comes next in the pattern begun by a, b, and c.

1.

a.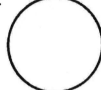

b.

c.

d.

2.

a.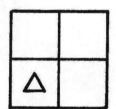

b.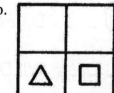

c.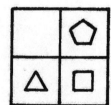

d.

From One Word to the Next

DIRECTIONS: For each line, rewrite the word from the line above, changing only the letter in the circle. Each word you write will be either the opposite or distinctly different from the word written on the left.

O L D   NEW

◯ __ __ __   HOT

◯ __ __ __   SHY

◯ __ __ __   DROP

__ __ __ ◯   FULL

◯ __ __ __   STUMP

__ ◯ __ __   TANNED

◯ __ __ __   OVERPRICED

__ __ ◯ __   DIFFERENT

◯ __ __ __   WILD

◯ __ __ __   UNKNOWN

◯ __ __ __   WENT

__ ◯ __ __   GO

Ⓗ O M E   AWAY

From *Word Benders Book A1.* For more activities like the one above, call 800-458-4849 for the store nearest you or to order directly. © 2002 Critical Thinking Books & Software • www.criticalthinking.com

Equations, Equations

DIRECTIONS: Place the given numbers in the squares so that each row and each column has the right answer.

1, 2, 3, 4, 5, 6, 8, 24

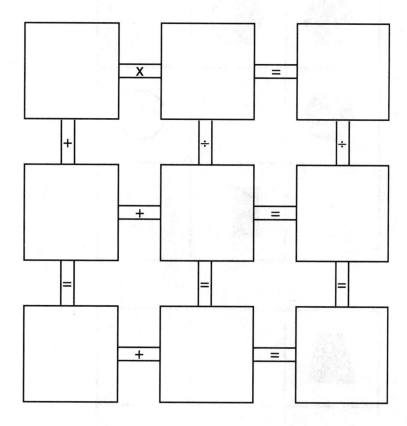

Fill in the Blanks

DIRECTIONS: Complete each matrix below by filling in the blanks with the figures that logically follow according to the patterns shown.

1.

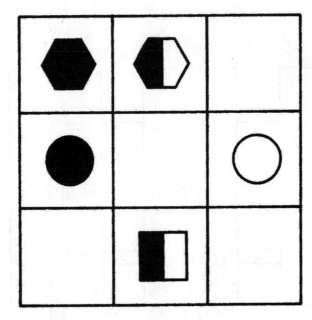

2.

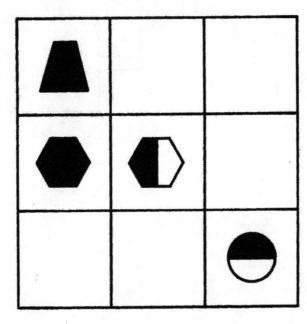

From *Figural Classifications Book A1.* For more activities like the one above, call 800-458-4849 for the store nearest you or to order directly. © 2002 Critical Thinking Books & Software • www.criticalthinking.com

It's Not Always What It Seems

PARTNER/GROUP
ACTIVITY

DIRECTIONS: The statement below is misleading—things are not as they first appear! Ask yes-or-no questions of your teacher (or someone who knows the answer) to get clues. Use as few questions as possible to figure out and describe the situation. Make every question count!

Even though his face was completely masked throughout the robbery, police were waiting for him when he arrived at his home. How did they know who he was and where he lived?

You Can Go for Miles and Miles and Miles

DIRECTIONS: Use a pencil or two pens with different colors of ink to do this puzzle. You will create two separate lines.

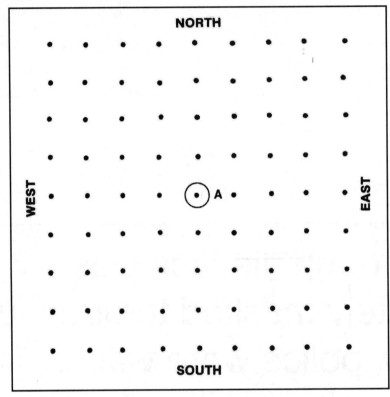

Note:
The space between two dots is equal to two miles.

1. Use one space to represent **two** miles. Draw the following path:
    Start at point **A** and proceed 4 miles south, then 6 mile east, then 12 miles north, then 10 miles west, and then 8 miles south.

    a.   How many miles have you traveled? _____

    b.   How many miles are you from point A? _____

    c.   What direction must you travel to return to point A? _____

2. Use one space to represent **two** miles. Draw the following path:
    Start at point **A** and proceed 6 miles west, then 4 miles north, then 2 miles west, then 10 miles south, and then 8 miles east.

    a.   How many miles have you traveled? _____

    b.   How many miles are you from point A? _____

    c.   What direction must you travel to return to point A? _____

Don't Lift Your Pencil!

DIRECTIONS: Try to trace the following figures without lifting your pencil. Intersecting or retracing lines are not permitted.

1.

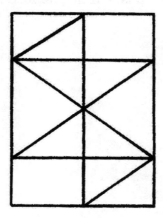

2.

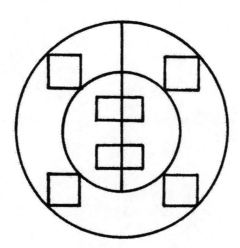

Talking About Tomatoes

Ms. Darby found out that she is allergic to tomatoes. Every time she eats something with tomatoes in it, she breaks out in a rash. Tell whether or not it is OK for her to eat the following foods. Circle the letters of the foods it is OK for her to eat.

a. catsup

b. mustard

c. pea soup

d. apple pie

e. chili

f. spaghetti sauce

g. vegetable soup

h. hamburgers

i. macaroni and cheese

From *Inductive Thinking Skills: Inferences Book A.* For more activities like the one above, call 800-458-4849 for the store nearest you or to order directly. © 2002 Critical Thinking Books & Software • www.criticalthinking.com

Block Figures

Each drawing represents a different view of the *same* block. Each block contains only one of each shape.

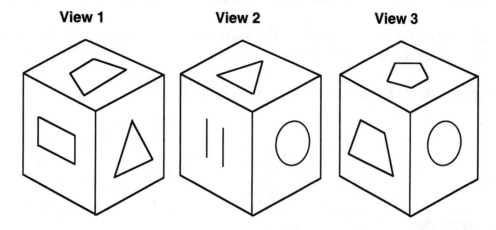

View 1   **View 2**   **View 3**

What shape is on the opposite side of each block? (Finish the grid below by crossing out the shapes that you know are not opposite; put a O in the box for shapes that are opposite.)

	TRAPEZOID	RECTANGLE	TRIANGLE	PARALLEL LINES	CIRCLE	PENTAGON
TRAPEZOID	X					
RECTANGLE		X				
TRIANGLE			X			
PARALLEL LINES				X		
CIRCLE					X	
PENTAGON						X

Figure: **Opposite figure:**

trapezoid   _____

rectangle   _____

triangle   _____

parallel lines   _____

circle   _____

pentagon   _____

Can You Be Sure?

ASSUME THE FOLLOWING IS TRUE

A. If school starts in the morning then Sheila and Donald will be late.

B. If Sheila and Donald are late then Mr. O'Connor will yell at Sheila and send Donald to the assistant principal's office.

C. School starts in the morning. Sheila is late.

QUESTIONS

1. Was Donald late?

2. Was Sandy yelled at?

3. Was Donald sent to the assistant principal's office?

From *Syllogisms Book A1.* For more activities like the one above, call 800-458-4849 for the store nearest you or to order directly. © 2002 Critical Thinking Books & Software · www.criticalthinking.com

Match Games

DIRECTIONS: Match the shape at the top to a form on the bottom row. The match must be the same size, color, and position.

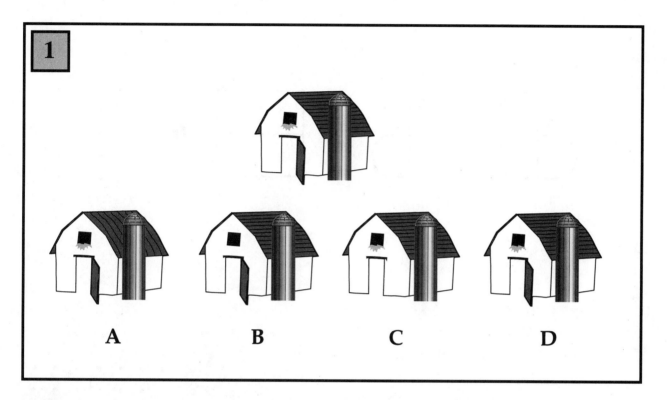

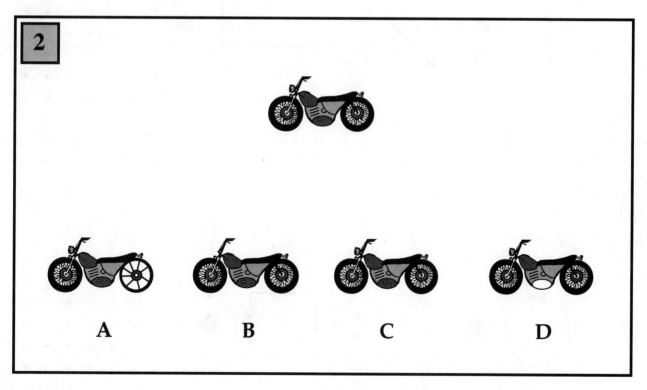

Think Ahead

DIRECTIONS: Observe the pattern from figure a to figure b. According to the same pattern, draw the figure for d that logically follows from figure c.

1.   a.   b.   c.   d.

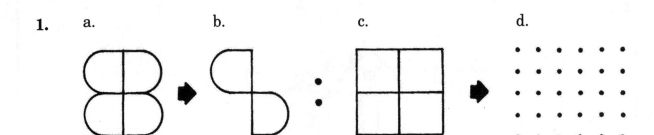

2.   a.   b.   c.   d.

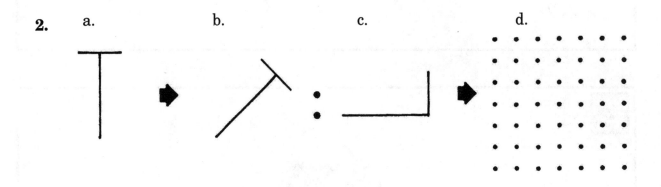

3.   a.   b.   c.   d.

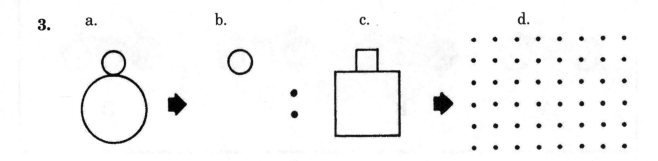

What Do You Think?

1. A stranger came to town last Monday. The people of the town didn't like his looks. That afternoon, Mrs. Maunry's dog got sick, and so did Mr. Towner's cat. The next day, the stranger walked under a ladder and nothing happened to him. But later that morning, the painter fell off the ladder and broke his leg. It's been one thing after another like that. That stranger brings bad luck wherever he goes.

   What's wrong with the speaker's reasoning?

2. Ruth is five years old. Her dad takes her to play in the park once a week. Each time she goes, there are trees in the park. She likes trees. She thinks it's nice that the trees come out just for her.

   What is wrong with Ruth's thinking?

Words, Words, and More Words

DIRECTIONS: On the line under each word, mark **1**, **2**, **3**, or **4** to indicate lowest to highest in size, degree, rank, or order. One (**1**) indicates the lowest and four (**4**) is the highest.

1.   foot   inch   meter   yard

       _____   _____   _____   _____

2.   dwarf   giant   average   tall

       _____   _____   _____   _____

3.   airplane   automobile   boat   bicycle

       _____   _____   _____   _____

4.   lake   ocean   pond

       _____   _____   _____

5.   hexagon   pentagon   square   triangle

       _____   _____   _____   _____

From *Verbal Sequences Book A1.* For more activities like the one above, call 800-458-4849 for the store nearest you or to order directly. © 2002 Critical Thinking Books & Software • www.criticalthinking.com

Think Literally!

DIRECTIONS: This verbal puzzle is really a common word or phrase. Write the phrase on the blank below.

EXAMPLE: | STAND ME | means **Stand By Me** since **Stand** is next to (by) **Me**.

BERNATE

_____

Four Fun Riddles

DIRECTIONS: Read all of the words of each riddle carefully, then write your answer on the lines provided. Reminder: The answer could be a word or a part of a word.

1.

My miss means you gave,
Your word you would do;
My mote means next year,
The next grade for you.

What am I? _____

2.

Alone I am evil,
Wicked, gross, and base;
With in I am high strung,
Plucked or stroked with grace.

What am I? _____

3.

My card has a picture,
Of him or her or him;
Alone I am a front,
That shines or else is grim.

What am I? _____

4.

My caps are heavy burdens,
Many are overcoming;
Alone I am the trait that,
You need to fix the plumbing.

What am I? _____

Figure It Out!

DIRECTIONS: Change the figures so that all of them fit the rule.

1. If the figure is a circle, then it is grey.

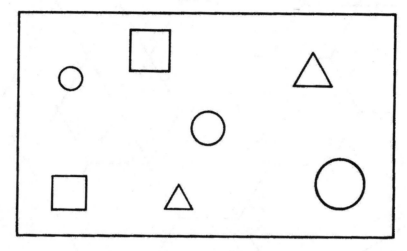

2. If the figure is grey, then it is a circle.

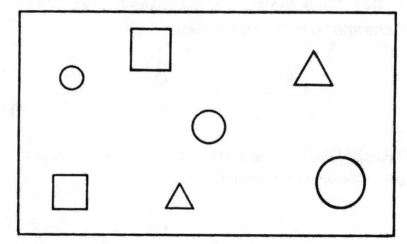

3. In problem 1, can you have
   a. a grey triangle? _____
   b. a striped circle? _____

4. In problem 2, can you have
   a. a grey triangle? _____
   b. a striped circle? _____

Finding the Correct Figure

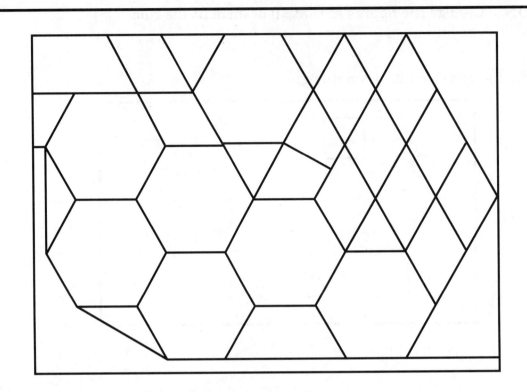

1 **DIRECTIONS:** Circle the answer that gives the number of ⬡ hexagons shown in the above design.

6	7	8	9
A	**B**	**C**	**D**

2 **DIRECTIONS:** Circle the answer that gives the number of ◇ diamonds shown in the above design.

10	11	12	13
A	**B**	**C**	**D**

3 **DIRECTIONS:** Circle the answer that gives the number of triangles shown in the above design.

8	9	10	11
A	**B**	**C**	**D**

The Spelling Contest

DIRECTIONS: Bobby, Jackie, Mickey, and Pat finished in first, second, third, and fourth places in a spelling contest. Figure out how each person did in the contest and whether the person is a boy or a girl. Use the chart to help you. (Put "X" on squares showing what is NOT true and put checks on squares showing what IS true.) Use the following clues.

1. The person who finished in first place does not know Jackie, but he knows her little brother.

2. Pat studied the spelling list with Mickey and the other girl, but both did better in the contest than he did.

3. Jackie did better in the contest than Mickey did.

	1st	2nd	3rd	4th
Bobby				
Jackie				
Mickey				
Pat				

Number Puzzlers

1. What is the 50th number in this sequence?

5, 11, 17, 23, 29, 35, 41, ...

Explain how you got your answer.

_____

_____

_____

2. Maria and Manuel are on the first floor of an office building that has 50 floors. Maria takes an elevator to the 25th floor. Manuel takes a different elevator that stops at the 5th floor.

Write an explanation, in terms of elevator travel, of how much farther Maria has traveled.

_____

_____

_____

_____

How Are These Words Related?

DIRECTIONS: Each line contains two words related to art or music. Think about the way the two words are alike. Underline the sentences(s) that is true of both words.

1. painting
   photograph
   a. Both are pictures.
   b. Both can be sold in art galleries.
   c. Both must represent real objects.

2. piano
   xylophone
   a. Both are musical instruments.
   b. Both have keys.
   c. Both are played by hitting with a stick.

3. marching band
   orchestra
   a. Both have horn players.
   b. Both have violin players.
   c. Both produce music.

4. artist
   composer
   a. Both are talented people.
   b. Both are involved in the arts.
   c. Both write music.

5. paints
   musical instruments
   a. Both are used by musicians
   b. Both can be used by talented people.
   c. Both can be held in the hand.

6. canvas
   music staff paper
   a. Both can be used to produce a creative work.
   b. Both have paint applied to them.
   c. Both are used to write music.

Some Are Alike, Some Are Different

DIRECTIONS: Each line below contains words. Four of the five words have something in common. The other word does not have this common factor. Write what the common factor is, and write the word that does not belong.

Example: a. nice, big, mean, kind, nasty

Common Factor	Doesn't Belong
ways to describe personality	big

1. dog, cat, canary, gerbil, tiger

Common Factor	Doesn't Belong

2. pen, crayon, pencil, chalk, hair

Common Factor	Doesn't Belong

3. green, red, warm, pink, blue

Common Factor	Doesn't Belong

4. driveway, wall, floor, ceiling, roof

Common Factor	Doesn't Belong

5. water, milk, meat, soda pop, coffee

Common Factor	Doesn't Belong

From *Basic Thinking Skills: Antonyms, Synonyms, Similarities, and Differences.* For more activities like the one above, call 800-458-4849 for the store nearest you or to order directly. © 2002 Critical Thinking Books & Software • www.criticalthinking.com

From One Word to the Next

DIRECTIONS: For each line, rewrite the word from the line above, changing only the letter in the circle. Each word you write will be either the opposite or distinctly different from the word written on the right.

POP   **C O R N**

APPLE   __ __ __ ◯

__ ◯ __ __   TAKER

◯ __ __ __   OR RABBIT

__ __ __ ◯   AND VOLUME

__ __ __ ◯   THE PAPER

__ __ __ __ ◯   , SET, GO

◯◯ __ __ __ __   AS SHE GOES

◯ __ __ __   PHONES

◯ __ __ __   AS A DOORNAIL

Ⓑ Ⓡ E A D   AND BUTTER

Time Is On Your Side

DIRECTIONS: Fill in the word that fits the sequence.

1. January, December, _____, October, _____,

   _____.

2. March, _____, July, September, _____, _____.

3. February, _____, October, _____, _____, October.

4. Thursday, Saturday, _____, _____, Friday,

   _____.

5. 9:30 a.m., _____, 11 a.m., _____, 12:30 p.m.,

   _____.

6. _____, 11:31 p.m., _____, 11:55 p.m., _____, 12:19 a.m.

7. 3:38 p.m., 3:30 p.m., _____, _____, 3:06 p.m.,

   _____.

What's a Good Analogy?

DIRECTIONS: Read the example of a good analogy. Then evaluate the analogy below.

A good analogy: Ezra and I always take the same test, and we always have the same answers for all the problems. So we should get the same grades.

Heather is three years old. She has several story books. They all have pictures in them. And all the stories are about make-believe people and animals. Heather has never seen any other books.

1. What does Heather probably think is true about all books?

2. Give some other examples of this kind of reasoning.

Think About Your Answer

1. If you take out six letters from the list below, the remaining letters will form a common English word. Find the word.

BSIANXLEATNTEARS

2. If you had only a match and entered a room containing an oil lamp, a fireplace, and a gas range, what would you light first? Why?

3. A farmer threw 9 ears of corn into the barn. A rat came in and left with 3 ears each day. It took the rat 9 days to take all of the corn. Why?

Four Fun Riddles

DIRECTIONS: Read all of the words of each riddle carefully, then write your answer on the lines provided. Reminder: The answer could be a word or a part of a word.

1.

My stroke you can get,
In sun without a hat;
Alone I am warmth,
Now, check the thermostat.

What am I? _____

2.

My poison is itchy,
And I'm a kind of tree;
And my name rhymes with poke,
Now can you think of me?

What am I? _____

3.

With N I'm the sound,
You make when you are sick;
Alone I'm the way,
You become tall and thick.

What am I? _____

4.

My back keeps the ball,
Close to the catcher;
My short is the one,
Who's a ball snatcher.

What am I? _____

ANSWER KEY

Page 1: Mystery Shapes

1

□

Page 2: It's a Date!

1. 18th
2. Sunday, Monday
3. 23rd
4. 29th
5. Tuesday
6. Saturday

Page 3: The Color of Fun

The given map should take at least 4 colors.

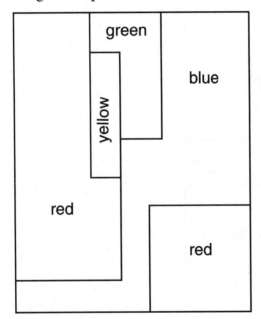

Page 4: Word Maker

Possible Answers

1. paint
2. more, lore, tore or sore
3. made
4. cone, done, bone or tone
5. gate, fate, late, mate or rate
6. unfit, fitted, fits

Page 5: Think Literally!

Don't worry about it

Page 6: Squares and More Squares

30 (16 1x1, 9 2x2, 4 3x3, 1 4x4)

Page 7: Turn the Triangles

1. A   2. A   3. C
    B C   B C   A B

Page 8: Word Puzzlers

1. BOY
2. MAN
3. LAD

Page 9: All Aboard!

1. (YES)
2. YES
3. NO
4. YES

Page 10: North, South, East, and West

1. east
2. circle
3. square
4.

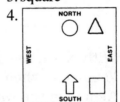

5. south
6. east
7. arrow
8. circle
9.

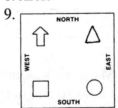

Page 11: What's Really Important

a. No
b. No

c. No (They already know he wants a dog, so when they asked for good reasons, they implied that this was not one of them.)

d. Yes

e. Yes

f. Yes

g. No

h. No

i. No

Page 12: Words That Match

1. rock clock
2. big pig
3. fish dish
4. wet jet
5. mouse house
6. blue flu
7. toad road
8. star jar
9. fire tire
10. neat street

Page 13: Get Your Brain in Gear

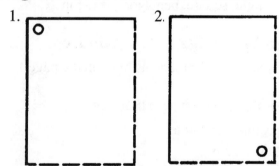

Page 14: Toothbrush Detective

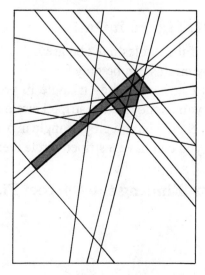

Page 15: What Comes Next?

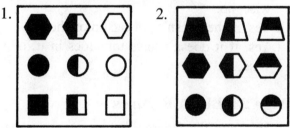

Page 16: From One Word to the Next

OLD	NEW
COLD	HOT
BOLD	SHY
HOLD	DROP
HOLE	FULL
POLE	STUMP
PALE	TANNED
SALE	OVERPRICED
SAME	DIFFERENT
TAME	WILD
FAME	UNKNOWN
CAME	WENT
COME	GO
HOME	AWAY

Page 17: Equations, Equations

4, 6, 24

1, 2, 3

5, 3, 8

Page 18: Follow the Pattern

Page 19: It's Not Always What It Seems

The robber wore a motorcycle helmet with a face guard that completely masked his features. However, he had not remembered that his name was painted on the back of his helmet, which victims noted and reported to the police.

Page 20: You Can Go for Miles and Miles

1. See graphic on next page

a. 40 miles

b. 4 miles

c. east
2. See graphic
   a. 30 miles
   b. 6 miles
   c. north

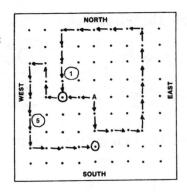

Page 21: Don't Lift Your Pencil!

1. 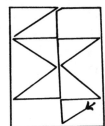 2.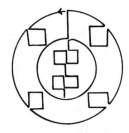

Page 22: Talking About Tomatoes

a. no
b. yes
c. yes
d. yes
e. Probably not, since most chili has tomatoes in it.
f. no
g. Yes, if it doesn't have tomatoes in it; otherwise, no.
h. Yes, if she doesn't put catsup on them.
i. Yes, if it doesn't have tomatoes in it; otherwise, no.

Page 23: Block Figures

Here are the figures that are opposite each other:
trapezoid—parallel lines
rectangle—circle
triangle—pentagon

Page 24: Can You Be Sure?

1. Yes, (C) tells us (A) will take place.
2. (?) The problem does not tell us anything about a person named Sandy.
3. Yes, (C) tells us that (A) will take place and (A) tells us that (B) will take place.

Page 25: Match Games

1. D
2. C

Page 26: Around the Squares

1d. 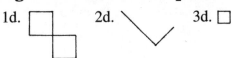   2d.   3d.

Page 27: What Do You Think?

1. The speaker is mistaking coincidence (or sequential events) for cause and effect.
2. Ruth apparently thinks that her coming to the park causes the trees to appear. She does not realize that the trees are there even when she does not go to the park.

Page 28: Words, Words, and More Words

1. inch, foot, yard, meter
2. dwarf, average, tall, giant
3. bicycle, boat, automobile, airplane (slow to fast)
4. pond, lake, ocean
5. triangle, square, pentagon, hexagon

Page 29: A Page Full of Squares

Hibernate ("Bernate" is high on the page.)

Page 30: Four Fun Riddles

1. promise, promote
2. vile, violin
3. face card, face
4. handicaps, handy

Page 31: Figure It Out!

1. All of the circles must be grey.
2. Only circles can be grey.
3. You can have a grey triangle in problem 1, but you cannot have a striped circle there.
4. You cannot have a grey triangle in problem 2, but you can have a striped circle there.

Page 32: Finding the Correct Figure

1. B
2. C
3. D

Page 33: The Spelling Contest

Pat is a boy (2). Then Mickey and one other person are girls (2). Jackie is a girl (1), so Bobby is a boy. A boy finished in first place (1), but he isn't Pat (2), so he is Bobby. Then Pat finished in fourth place (2). Jackie finished in second place and Mickey finished in third place (3).

NAME	SEX	PLACE
Bobby	boy	first
Jackie	girl	second
Mickey	girl	third
Pat	boy	fourth

Page 34: Number Puzzlers

1. 299. The pattern involves a difference of 6 between adjacent terms of the sequence. Add 6 to 5, getting 11, then add 6 to 11, getting 17, then add 6 to 17, getting 23, etc., until 6 has been added 50 times, ending in 299. Answer explanations will vary.
2. Maria has traveled 6 times as far as Manuel. Going from the first floor to the second floor is one elevator move. Going from the second to the third floor is a second elevator move. Going from the third to the fourth floor is a third elevator move. Going from the fourth floor to the fifth is a fourth elevator move. So, going from the first to the fifth floor takes 4 elevator moves. Similarly, there would be 24 elevator moves going from the first to the 25th floor. $\frac{24}{4} = 6$. Answer explanations will vary.

Page 35: How Are These Words Related?

1. a and b
2. a and b
3. a and c
4. a and b
5. b and c
6. a

Page 36: Some Are Alike, Some Different

1. pets; tiger OR 4-legged animals; canary
2. writing instruments; hair
3. colors; warm OR 4-letter words; red
4. parts of a building; driveway
5. liquids; meat

Page 37: From One Word to the Other

POP   CORN
APPLE   CORE
         CARE TAKER
         HARE OR RABBIT
          AREA AND VOLUME
          READ THE PAPER
          READY, SET, GO
           STEADY AS SHE GOES
            HEAD PHONES
            DEAD AS A DOORNAIL
            BREAD AND BUTTER

Page 38: Time Is On Your Side

1. November, September, August
2. May, November, January
3. June, February, June
4. Monday, Wednesday, Sunday
5. 10:15 a.m., 11:45 a.m., 1:15 p.m.
6. 11:19 p.m., 11:43 p.m., 12:07 a.m.
7. 3:22 p.m., 3:14 p.m., 2:58 p.m.

Page 39: What's a Good Analogy?

a. She probably thinks that all books have pictures in them and have stories about make-believe characters.
b. Answers will vary.

Page 40: Think About Your Answer

1. BANANA. Take out S, I, X, L, E, T, T, E, R, S.
2. The match—so you can light a longer-lasting light source.
3. The rat took its own 2 ears and 1 ear of corn each time it left the barn. If the rat carried only 1 ear of corn per day, it would take the rat 9 days to remove the 9 ears of corn from the barn.

Page 41: More Fun Riddles

1. <u>heat</u>stroke, <u>heat</u>
2. poison <u>oak</u>, <u>oak</u>
3. <u>groan</u>, <u>grow</u>
4. back<u>stop</u>, short<u>stop</u>

ACTIVITY/PRODUCT REFERENCE

PAGE NUMBER	ACTIVITY TITLE	SERIES TITLE	OTHER ACTIVITIES FROM THE SERIES
1	Mystery Shape	Language Smarts	p. 12
2	It's a Date!	Thinking About Time	p. 38
3	The Color of Fun	Math Ties	p. 23
4	Word Maker	Verbal Sequences	p. 28
5	Think Literally!	Think-A-Grams	p. 29
6	Squares and More Squares	Classroom Quickies	
7	Turn the Triangles	Inductive Thinking Skills	pp. 11, 13, 15
8	Word Puzzlers	Creative Problem Solving	
9	All Aboard!	Visual Logic	p. 31
10	North, South, East, and West	Thinking Directionally	p. 20
11	What's Really Important	Inductive Thinking Skills	pp. 7, 13, 15
12	Words That Match	Language Smarts	p. 1
13	Get Your Brain in Gear	Inductive Thinking Skills	pp. 7, 13, 15
14	Toothbrush Detective	Brain Stretchers	p. 21
15	What Comes Next?	Inductive Thinking Skills	pp. 7, 11, 13
16	From One Word to the Next	Word Benders	p. 37
17	Equations, Equations	Cranium Crackers	
18	Fill in the Blanks	Figural Classifications	
19	It's Not Always What It Seems*	A Case of Red Herrings	
20	You Can Go for Miles and Miles	Thinking Directionally	p. 10
21	Don't Lift Your Pencil!	Brain Stretchers	p. 14
22	Talking About Tomatoes	Inductive Thinking Skills	pp. 27, 39
23	Block Figures	Math Ties	p. 3
24	Can You Be Sure?	Syllogisms	
25	Match Games	Visual Perceptual Skill Building	p. 32
26	Think Ahead	Figural Analogies	
27	What Do You Think?	Inductive Thinking Skills	pp. 22, 39
28	Words, Words, More Words	Verbal Sequences	p. 4
29	Think Literally!	Think-A-Grams	p. 7
30	Four Fun Riddles	Dr. DooRiddles	p. 41
31	Figure It Out!	Visual Logic	p. 9
32	Finding the Correct Figure	Visual Perceptual Skill Building	p. 25
33	The Spelling Contest	Mind Benders®	
34	Number Puzzlers	Scratch Your Brain	p. 40
35	How Are These Words Related?	Building Thinking Skills®	
36	Some Are Alike, Some Different	Basic Thinking Skills	
37	From One Word to the Next	Word Benders	p. 16
38	Time Is on Your Side	Thinking About Time	p. 2
39	What's a Good Analogy?	Inductive Thinking Skills	pp. 22, 27
40	Think About Your Answer	Scratch Your Brain	p. 34
41	Four Fun Riddles	Dr. DooRiddles	p. 30

* Partner/Group Activity